What Is in Your Pillow?

What Is in Your Pillow?

Titilayo Akinniyi

ISBN: Hardcover   9781796025385
               Softcover   9781796025378
               eBook   9781796025361

Scripture quotations marked NKJV are taken from the New King James Version. Copyright © 1982 by Thomas Nelson, Inc. Used by permission. All rights reserved.

The views expressed in this work are solely those of the author and do not necessarily reflect the views of the publisher, and the publisher hereby disclaims any responsibility for them.

Any people depicted in stock imagery provided by Getty Images are models, and such images are being used for illustrative purposes only.
Certain stock imagery © Getty Images.

Print information available on the last page.

Rev. date: 03/30/2019

To order additional copies of this book, contact:
Xlibris
1-888-795-4274
www.Xlibris.com
Orders@Xlibris.com
794949

CONTENTS

Dedication

This book is dedicated to God Almighty and to all parents. It is my prayer that our night time in life shall be peaceful in Jesus name.

Acknowledgment

All thanks and glory to the Almighty God the Giver of Divine inspiration. I will always be grateful to Your mercies in my life.

My husband Engineer Olusegun Akinniyi, I am truly grateful for your support and Godly counsel while I was writing this book. The time taken to edit this book is much appreciated.

My sincere appreciation goes to my children Oluwakemi, Olayinka and Oluwatobiloba Akinniyi for your words of encouragement and prayers for me to do what God wants me to do. I am blessed to have you all by my side.

My senior brother Mr Ajibola Fatai Lawal, I say thank you for being there when you were most needed. Your role in my life contributed in no small way to who I am today.

Thank you all for being there for me. God bless and make you instruments of positive change in His Kingdom in Jesus name.

CHAPTER 1

What is a pillow?

A pillow is a cloth bag stuffed with soft material and used to support the head and neck when sleeping or reclining. Apart from providing comfort when sleeping, there are other uses for a pillow including therapy, decoration and play.

A pillow is an essential part of a complete bed set at homes.

It brings out the beauty of the bed as a complete set. Children, like a pillow make the family complete. It does not matter if the children are biological or adopted, the promise of God for all is fruitfulness all round. His word says that you shall serve The Lord your God and He shall bless you, and none shall be barren. Remember that the gifts and the calling of God are without repentance. He said He will not change the word that has gone out of His mouth <u>concerning our destinies</u>. (underlined words are mine)

Exodus 23:25-26

25 "So you shall serve the Lord your God, and
He will bless your bread and your water. And I
will take sickness away from the midst of you.

26 No one shall suffer miscarriage or be barren
in your land; I will fulfil the number of your
days.

It is not enough to have children, but it is Godly to have
beautiful children.

Our children shall be beautiful all the days of their lives
in Jesus name. Some children are beautiful in the morning
of their lives but end up as thorns in the flesh of the parents
and society in their later years bringing shame and discomfort
to the parents. Ours shall not be so in Jesus name. The plan
and purpose of God shall stand in their lives in Jesus name.
The spirit that destroys lives shall not locate our children and
children's children.

Godly and goodly children add beauty to the lives of parents.
A successful child will always make the parents look beautiful
amid friends or in any gathering.

A pillow that is well or perfectly selected, brings comfort to
the user. A poorly selected pillow most times is a source of pain
and discomfort to the user.

If every parent is mindful of the way the children are
trained, the children will turn out to be a source of comfort to
the parents especially in the night of their lives. A child that is

always involved in trouble cannot make the night of the lives of the parents comfortable. It will be a very restless night full of worries like Job in the bible. He was always worried about his children anytime they are out of his sight. Our children should make our lives comfortable anywhere we or they may be. We should not be in panic mode every second thinking of what may be going on in their lives. A child who is not properly trained by his parents will be nothing but a source of discomfort one way or the other. A child who lacks moral value has nothing to offer the parents in old age except troubles. If we refuse to put into our pillow the right fill, we will have ourselves to blame.

CHAPTER 2

Components of a pillow

A pillow consists of two main parts:

 i. The pillow cover which is the outer part. This is the readily visible part of the pillow.

 ii. The pillow inserts. This is the inside or inner that is inserted in the cover.

In addition to the two main parts, the edges of a pillow cover may have welt, trim or a flange sewn onto them for additional decoration.

THE PILLOW COVER

Understanding a pillow's parts is important so you can order pillows to your exact specifications.

The cover is the first part of the pillow that shows its beauty. It is the first point of contact for the hand and eyes.

The choice of material and colour for the pillow cover should be taken seriously. If the colour is not attractive, no one would like to go near to check how soft or hard it is.

Eyes are always attracted to beautiful things like colour, shape, design and textures. There are some textures that could be felt by the eyes even before the hands encounter the object.

Some colours are tangy to the eyes while some are cool and inviting to the eyes. If you are in the pillow or fashion business, you will be conversant with the reaction of human eyes to colours.

Research has shown that we are able to see different colours because of visionary cone cells in the retina of our eyes. Each cone cell is sensitive to one of four major colours – red, green, blue and orange.

Most people have three cone cells while some, mainly women have four. This is probably why some women have better colour vision than men.

Talking about the home, a woman can easily detect the shade or colour of troubles in her home. When a person says, 'I can see the dark side of this situation', it does not really mean the situation is physically painted in a dark colour. It basically means the person feel that the situation is bad. Women can feel the shade of a strange woman trying to invade her home even without being told. When a woman tells her husband to be careful of a friend or a woman who is trying to waggle her way into the man's life, it means she can see the shade with her God given fourth cone cells.

People are grouped into categories according to the number of cones: trichromats, and tetrachromats.

Most people are trichromatic, meaning that they have three types of cone cells — red, blue, and green — and information from the different types of cones combines to produce colour perception. Since each type of cone enables the eye to distinguish approximately 100 shades, the average human combines those exponentially and can see about 1 million shades.

Those with four cones are the tetrachromats and can see about 100 million shades because of the additional orange colour cone cells.

From this, we can see that the Almighty God Himself made us to be able to see from afar the colour that someone is made of. That is how powerful God has made us to be.

So, the pillow in our lives can be perceived by others just by looking.

We must therefore invest quality time and effort into the choice of colour that our pillow is made of. The choice of the colour should be prayerfully considered.

Other thing to consider in choosing the outer part of our pillow is the fabric texture.

The texture is the feeling of the fabric to the hands. Harsh texture drives people away from the fabric. A soft and smooth texture attracts people of good intention. When something feels soft, you do not want to leave quickly. You want to enjoy it a little longer.

Washing a thing with water makes the outer part cleaner. When you wash with the word of God it makes both the inner and outer parts cleaner to show forth the glory of God.

The words that we speak to our children wash the outer and inner parts of their lives and the result shows outwardly.

Helpers of destiny are attracted to our pillows (children) when the outward texture is soft and clean.

Ephesians 5:26

26 that He might sanctify and cleanse her with
the washing of water by the word,

THE PILLOW INSERT

This is the stuffing or content of the cloth bag that forms the outer cover of our pillow. Pillow fill comes in different forms and different materials. It ranges from Downing pillow fill to Microbead pillow fill.

The choice of pillow fill depends on the level of comfort you desire and most importantly on how much money you want to invest in it.

As much as the outer part of the pillow is important, so much more the content is of greater importance. Sometimes, the outer cover could be over looked if the content is right. Have you heard of the saying, "Do not judge a book by its cover"?

Some pillows are beautiful and attractive to the eyes, but inside, there is nothing to write home about. Good container with bad content.

Filling our pillow requires adequate knowledge of the type of materials needed for the desired comfort that we want from the pillow. This goes beyond the outward look. It is a step further in the right direction for the pillow to be useful. What is the use of a thing that we spent so much time to make and at the end of the day it is not useful for its intended purpose? The scripture says, if salt loses its taste, it is thrown to the ground and trodden upon. It is considered a waste and could be frustrating.

The character of a pillow depends on its fills. A pillow could be soft, firm or comfortable.

Matthew 5: 13

13 You are the salt of the earth; but if the salt loses its flavour, how shall it be seasoned? It is then good for nothing but to be thrown out and trampled underfoot by men.

Let us look a closer look at some of the pillow fills.

Down Pillow Filling

This is the undercoating of a bird's feathers called down. It is the bottom, fluffy part of a bird's feather. It is very soft, better than synthetic fill and expensive.

Down pillow fill holds its shape well, resulting in good support for the head and neck. That is comfort.

Polyester Fiberfil Pillow Filling

This is cheaper than the down pillow fill but is considered potentially hazardous to health and the environment due to its chemical composition. The filling material contains chemicals like formaldehyde, benzene, toluene and other toxins.

Shredded Memory Foam Pillow Filling

This is manufactured using polyurethane and several other chemicals which makes it to emit strong chemical odour. This is considered unhealthy and makes people feel uncomfortable.

Buckwheat Hull Pillow Filling

This is firm, can be shaped as desired and is breathable, making it the ideal pillow fill. It conforms perfectly to the shape of the head and neck making the user feel comfortable. The fact that the material promotes air flow keeps the user cool.

Microbead pillow filling

Microbeads are also called "uniform polymer particles." They are the synthetic alternative to buckwheat hulls and share a lot of the same characteristics which includes promoting air flow and keeping the user cool at night.

CHAPTER 3

A Word for the Fathers

A father is the male parent of a child. Fathers are pillars in the development of their children's emotional well-being. Children look up to their fathers for physical and emotional security. An involved father promotes inner growth and strength in a child. Have you witnessed how a child feels when the father appears at school functions, how happy and full of confidence the child suddenly becomes? A good father should know that he is a pillar of strength, support and discipline in his children's lives.

THE DEMANDS OF FATHERHOOD

The role of the father is very significant in the life of a child. The bible says in proverbs 17:6

Proverbs 17:6

6 Children's children are the crown of old men,
And the glory of children is their father.

A father should be the role model for the child. He is the authority representing God in his home. In the spiritual hierarchy, after Christ comes the man. Where the head is missing, the whole body is lifeless. A lifeless home cannot showcase the glory of God. From the scripture above, the glory of children is their father. Let me appeal to men, who plan to have children but are not ready for the responsibilities of being a father. I would strictly advise that you have a rethink. What use is it to you and society if you churn out babies who, later in life, become pains in the fabric of the society.

Do not leave your responsibilities to the woman who forsook everything to partner with you as your help meet in achieving the plan of God for your life. Remember, she had to drop her father's name to take on yours. She deserves some respect and honour.

Raising Godly children that will eventually become your pillows for a restful night requires joint effort, time and sacrifice from both of you. Do not bury your head in your job and expect the children to be properly brought up by their mother alone. Life was not designed by God to be that way. Your wife is your helpmeet. She was not created to do your assignment for you but to support you and do it with you.

Create time out of your busy schedule to nurture the gift that God gave both of you. Be there for your children and let them see God in you through your care and your relationship with their mother and other people. Remember I said before that a child who did not receive any love or care will not be able to give it to others. The 'others' in my last statement include you, the child's parent. Fathers, do not be absent in your children's lives. It may be too late for you to win them over after many years of abandoning them in your pursuit of money for their care.

It has been discovered in some parts of the western world that the absence of fathers is the primary reason why many male children end up in prison. Some children are not in physical prisons but in spiritual ones. What do you say about a child who commits suicide because he is being bullied at school? When a father is missing in the life of a child, a vacuum is created which, in many cases is filled with evil imaginations that could lead to suicide. If the child has a father that he can open to about anything that is affecting him or her, the good counsel of the father will most likely rescue the child from evil thoughts. Children may not remember the colour or price of the dresses or shirts you bought for them when they were growing up, but they will never forget your presence at their sport events and birthday celebrations.

No matter how many times you tell them that you love them, your absence in their lives negates all that. Have an imprint of your love and care in the hearts of your children. As you do that, you are stuffing your pillow with the best filling for a good night's rest. Remember, it is what you are doing that these children are going to repeat in their own families when they have theirs. Do not sow a bad seed for the coming generations. A caring father must be available to show what a good man is like, especially to her daughters as they prepare for their future relationships with the men they will be married to.

You as a father must also be a good model for your son. He is the one that will carry on your name after you have finished your assignment on earth. How do you want your posterity to look like? Or should I say, what do you want the next generation to say about you? Leave good seeds so that generations after you can say you are of blessed memory. Some fathers are not of blessed memory; they are completely forgotten after they passed away and when remembered, their descendants curse them. That shall not be your portion in Jesus name.

Fathers please be there for your children. No one can be their father except you. It does not matter how much a school teacher puts in to fill the father role in your child's life, he cannot be like you. Somebody else can only try but cannot be you. The child carries your DNA.

Proverbs 10:7

7 The memory of the righteous is blessed,

But the name of the wicked will rot.

Teach your children to be responsible in life so you can eat good fruit in your night time. Teach them to be diligent in what they do. Be a hardworking father. Show your son how to love a woman by loving his mother. This will help him when he gets married. He watches what you do or how you treat his mother and that is exactly what he will do when he marries. Little wonder then that men whose fathers practised polygamy tend to follow the same pattern. I believe this is the law of mentorship.

It will take the intervention of God to destroy the yoke in the life of the son.

Plan for the number of children that you can care for. Do not give birth to children that you cannot care for because you have a rich relative. Relatives will turn your children to slaves and these children will curse you. Some people rely on neighbours to look after their children for them. Why that? Have you not heard of neighbours sexually abusing little girls? I will deal with this matter when I speak to mothers.

In a film titled Capernaum. A 12-year-old boy had to fend for himself and his junior ones because of the laziness of his father. This represents a reversal of role in the household. The bible commands every man to provide for his household and if he does not, he is equated to an unbeliever who does not believe in God and will not be able to taste the manifold blessings of God. With the role reversal, this boy had no choice than to take a step that he deemed was okay for him. With the help of someone, he charged his parents to court because of negligence and irresponsibility. A child suing the parents? That was exactly what happened. When asked by the Judge why he sued his parents, the boy's simple response was that he hated both parents for giving birth to him. Then he asked the court to speak to his parents to stop having children. Surprised? I was surprised too. It was very pathetic too, but do you blame him? He was expecting better care and love from the parents especially the father, but he never received any care and love. What will be our report to the God of heaven who looked unto us and counted us worthy to nurture these children in His way so that we may raise many strong nations that will proclaim His kingdom? Will we give a disappointing report? You and I shall not disappoint God in Jesus name.

Fathers, do not through your passiveness appear as dead while you are still living. Be active in the lives of your children. Be involved in their lives. Do not leave them to do whatever suits them. One day they will cause you shame openly if you don't care for them. Whatever you do in the hidden shall be made manifest in the open. Shame is not easy to wipe out from your life or family. A good man leaves an inheritance for his children's children. Leaving shame makes a father a bad man.

Ephesians 6:4

And you, fathers, do not provoke your children
to wrath, but bring them up in the training and
admonition of the Lord.

Proverbs 10:5

He who gathers in summer is a wise son;

He who sleeps in harvest is a son who causes
shame

No father shall be put to shame in Jesus name. All your labour shall be fully rewarded by God. Being a Godly and goodly father takes more than normal effort. There are many other things seeking for a man's attention. God must be your source of help in being the father that God wants you to be. God gave the assignment, He will supply the strength in Jesus' name. Look unto Him always. Do not train your children in the way and manner that your friends are training theirs. You are your children's father and you are not meant to co-father your children with others. Never compare your children with any other child or children. This makes the child to lose trust in you and himself. This is dangerous.

2 Corinthians 10:12

12 For we dare not class ourselves or compare
ourselves with those who commend themselves.
But they, measuring themselves by themselves,
and comparing themselves among themselves,
are not wise.

I recently watched an episode of a television program called "A date with your ex". In this episode, two people who had previously separated got together in the same room to see if they could resolve their differences or put a final closure to it. While they were trying to figure out what made them split, the man tried to apologise to the woman claiming that his behaviour was influenced by his father's behaviour when he was growing up. He said his father abandoned him and his leading to a fatherly love vacuum in his life. There was no father to attend his school activities and birthday celebrations. He was emotionally injured and made up his mind never to be fully involved in any relationship to avoid another pain in case the person abandons him like his father did.

The cost of not being a responsible father is enormous. We can see how a father's irresponsibility has led to pain in other people's lives. The knock-on effect of a father's irresponsibility has affected this innocent lady. Living without a responsible father has engendered an act of revenge and show of bitterness.

You never know how painful it is to be jilted, or for a man to tell a woman that he is no longer interested in their relationship. It is shameful and disappointing.

Men, help us! Destinies are being destroyed through the irresponsible attitudes of some fathers to the children that God has given them.

What qualifies us to be fruitful in our bodies? What makes us to be chosen to be parents?

Nothing, but the grace and mercies of God.

CHAPTER 4

A Word For The Mothers

God in His love and mercy decided to pick you out of many to honour you with marriage. Getting married is every woman's dream and not only that, but also to be called a mother. Remember, you can be a mother to either your biological child or an adopted one.

God's divine purpose for a woman is to be the Help that is meet for a man. His agenda is for a woman to have Godly seed that will take over from the old generation and continue God's purpose on earth. I am not sure God wants to re-create man all over again. He did it once and that was it. I believe that was why He preserved Noah's family and all the animals two by two. Procreation is part of the helpmeet assignment. If it was possible for the man to be pregnant and have children all by himself, then, the woman would not have been needed. I believe the other animals or all of God's creatures were made male and female because the bible says that God saw that none of these animals could be comparable with man. Adam was alone. None looked like him physically and none could bear him what will looked like him. The fruit trees in the garden of Eden all bore their kinds.

Genesis 1:11

11 Then God said, "Let the earth bring forth grass, the herb that yields seed, and the fruit tree that yields fruit according to its kind, whose seed is in itself, on the earth"; and it was so.

What is the role of the woman in filling the pillow? This is an interesting question I would like us to consider next.

Proverbs 14:1

The wise woman builds her house,

But the foolish pulls it down with her hands.

As I have said, you are the builder of the home if you are wise according to the scripture. Wisdom that is heavenly only comes from God.

James 3:17

But the wisdom that is from above is first pure, then peaceable, gentle, willing to yield, full of mercy and good fruits, without partiality and without hypocrisy.

I challenge you to be that woman endued with God's wisdom to build a lasting home and fill your pillow with the right fills.

A builder must know what the purpose of a house is. How many rooms or what type of load is it going to carry? What is the best foundation for the house? What will the house look like? That is, its shape and colour. The builder should be able to determine to some extent the items needed to fill the rooms to make them habitable.

Woman as the builder of her home must know who she is and the reason for her existence. She should have complete knowledge of who she is in God and who she is in herself. What you do not have you cannot give. A woman must first build herself to be able to build the house that will contain hers and others.

INVEST IN YOUR PILLOW

Here is a list of some important things we need to consider when building a house:

- Time
- Resources
- Sacrifice
- Planning.
- Knowledge

Time

It takes time to build a house. There is a scheduled time for erecting each building element and this time must be maintained for the entire building to be completed on time. Procrastination is an enemy of time. Though everything in life has its time, it is wise to factor in the importance of good time management. Time is a resource that must be spent wisely, otherwise, a trade-off will have to be made. If you are in a hurry to build a house, you must be ready to spend more money because you may need to use some special building materials like rapid hardening cement. Building our children up has been likened to building a good home, but that does not mean we can or should turn the character-building process into an emergency or microwave oven process. If you are in a rush to train your child who can only take in bite-sized information per time, you may end up destroying the child. Your objective may not be achieved that way.

I did say before that you can start speaking life into your child from the womb or even start declaring God's blessing on the child while you are still unmarried.

But sometimes it looks like nothing is changing despite all the declarations. Do not give up. Keep doing what needs to be done and surely you will see the result that will gladden your heart. Remember time is an asset. Use it and never be tired of using it. It takes time for the strokes of an axe to split the wood or fell a tree. What splits the wood is not normally the first stroke. You keep striking the tree until one last stroke gives you the desired result. Giving up early or looking back puts us in a complaint mode which is contrary to what God is expecting from us. Have you ever imagined how many times God has tried to say the same thing to you before you finally got the message He was trying to pass across? God the Almighty does not give up on us at any time, we are the ones who give up on God.

Galatians 6:9

9 And let us not grow weary while doing good,
for in due season we shall reap if we do not lose
heart.

A mother needs to be around or available for the children. The job of parenting is not something to be delegated. Why should a mother place the destiny of her child into the hands of house helps and friends or relatives? Did you consult them before having the child to make them realise that they will be co-workers with you in the training of your child?

Do not over burden your older children in helping you to take care of the younger ones. As much as you would like the older children to know how to care for the younger ones, don't turn them to the nannies or child minders. Your children are your children, don't pass your responsibility to your older children. A house that is overloaded may collapse. Do not allow your older children to collapse emotionally under the heavy load of taking care of their younger siblings. Be responsible for your pillow.

<u>Galatians 6:5</u>

For each one shall bear his own load.

Every woman should be responsible for her children. She carried their pregnancies and must be ready to carry them through life spiritually and emotionally. No retirement age in motherhood. The child will be her pillow particularly in the night of her life. I read somewhere that the First Lady of the United states of America, Melanie Trump, never employed house helps when raising her child. That is highly commendable. Pastor (Mrs) Faith Oyedepo, wife of the founder of the Living Faith Church Worldwide (a.k.a Winners Chapel International), personally picked up her children from Sunday school class after service every Sunday. I remember meeting her several times while picking up my children at the Raji Oba Street Campus, the then headquarters of the church in Lagos Nigeria. That is great example. She did not use her status as a Pastor and wife of the Founder of the church as an excuse to leave her pillows in the hands of others. Nobody knows how to handle your pillow better than you. You are the only one who knows the best pillow fill that will give you the comfort you desire. Others will only fill your pillow to meet their own requirements or perhaps intentionally fill it with material that will make you uncomfortable. Be responsible for your future. Your future is yours, not someone else's.

As mothers, what examples are we showing our children? If you depend on drivers to take your children to school always because you can afford it, there will come a time when the child too can afford a driver and will not be willing to drive you around. You will reap what you sow. Take time to bond with your children.

Some mothers take their time to train other people's children but neglect theirs. If you have people living with you or you have house helps that do all the cleaning and cooking and you refuse to let your children participate in the chores, you will pay for it later in life. When your daughter gets married and starts to call you to enquire about how much salt to add to her husband's food, everyone will know the type of mother you are. If your son's wife is tired or pregnant and is unable to cook and your son cannot fill in to prepare food for his wife and little children, then, there is a big problem. If your son's house is in disarray because his wife is sick or pregnant, and your son does not know what to do in the house, then, your daughter-in-law will criticize you.

Let us be conscious of the future. Someone says, for you to achieve great things in life, you must always have the picture of the end (that is, the future) in your heart. Then pursuing that picture becomes easier.

Do your best to fill the pillow well with lasting and comfortable fill. If not for yourself, do it for others especially the family that will inherit your daughter or son in marriage.

Remember that woman was created because she was needed. You are the beautiful, hopeful and glorious future of a family or nation or even the world. You are very important in building the nation. Let us do our best as women to be builders indeed.

One thing that keeps bothering me is the attitude of some of us trying to compete with our husbands financially. There is a big problem when a woman starts to say," my husband has 20 million dollars, I must match or exceed his achievement". Some women operate on the philosophy that what a man can do, a woman can do even better. There are limits to what a woman can do and cannot do. There is no way a woman can impregnate another woman. At least until now we have not seen that. God knows why He made a man and why He created a woman. Do not misunderstand me. It is possible for a woman to be richer than her husband. But things can change if the man discovers God's plan for him as the head of his home, the provider and Christ's representative in that home. Situations such as loss of job or a downturn in business may make the man to be lesser than his wife financially, but with God and diligence on the man's part, he will soon see himself soaring higher financially.

It is my prayer that no family will experience reversal of its God-ordained roles in Jesus name. By reversal of roles, I mean a situation where the woman turns out to be the bread winner for the family. The head of the family shall remain the head financially in Jesus name.

Woman, do not compete with your husband at the expense of your children's future.

Neglecting your future pillow to run after dollars or any currency is not the best at all. I ask myself this simple question. After all the running around like headless chicken, looking for money that was not lost, and abandoning my primary assignment of taking good care of my husband and God given children, what next? A time will come that the body will say to me, enough is enough; the running around must stop. Who do I fall back to? The family that I neglected? The home that I left in ruin? Nothing covers nakedness like good people, especially family. You cannot buy good family in the market. If you sell your family cheap by neglecting them, no one will be ready to take care of you when you most need them. Do you wonder why some children forget what their parents are going through in their old age? Many parents are left to suffer by their children who should have been their covering cloth at old age.

In fact, while you are running the rat race for money, it is most likely that a strange woman will be working her way into the vacant position in your home. You will probably say 'God forbid', but you need to forbid it yourself. There is no vacuum in life. The child that you do not have time for will find solace outside the home. The type of fills that will be inside him or her may not be what will give you the comfort you desire in your night time.

Have you ever wondered why some children are so detached from their parents? There was no bonding at all. Instead of bonding with their nonchalant parents, such children bond with television, computer games and all sorts. Do not indulge your children to the point of destroying their lives. Latest computer games will soon become outdated. What lasts long is the value injected in the child.

I remember when I was still young in marriage and I was looking for a job as a civil engineer because I wanted to practice in my field of training. My husband, who is also a civil engineer, was always away from home, sometimes spending up to two weeks in the oil field or tank farm. I made up my mind to put my career on hold to build my pillows, or shall I say our pillows. What I did was to go into business that would allow me to be there for my children. I did not have the luxury of mother/daughter relationship while I was growing up because of parents' divorce. Growing up in a broken home is not a good thing for any child. Please pray before you say I do to a man. The problem may not really come from the man, it could be from his family. Do not only pray to marry a rich man or for the man alone, pray about everything and everyone that is connected to him. His parents, friends, extended family members and even colleagues at work can have a great influence on your marriage. Someone would say, but my prayer covers my husband. Pray, even when you are still single. Create a mental picture of the future you want for your family and pray accordingly.

Marry who God wants you to marry. Do not marry because of material things. All these will go, and what will you be left with?

When I was growing up, I lived with several step mothers from different cultures across my native country Nigeria. Some of them were literally my age mates. It was terrible.

As a single Christian lady, it is your duty to seek God's face before you go on the sacred journey of marriage. I was not born again when I got married but I knew there was a God somewhere who cared for anyone who called on Him. I said earlier on that I spoke to God about my expectations for a husband. God is too faithful to fail. Despite my rough childhood and lack of good counsel or good example from the people around me, God met my expectations. I grew up in a house where swear words were the last words you heard before you went to bed and the first words you heard when you woke up. My mother never had a chance to show me the way. She was subjected to a life of torture in her distressed marriage and finally sent packing because of strange women. But God still found me and made His face to shine on me. He is not a respecter of persons.

Resources

Another thing I would like to mention about filling your pillow is resources. This is in the form of God's word. You might have thought about money when I first mentioned the word 'resources. Yes, you are right. A woman should have her own thing when it comes to money. You do not want to start asking your husband for money every time to buy little things like ice cream or school materials like note books and pencils for your children. There is a kind of respect from the children when they see how financially responsible their mother is.

I made up my mind to have a lasting impact on the lives of my children by personally paying a little part of their school fees even though the provisions have been made by my husband. I want to matter in their lives not only by praying or instilling Godly values in them but by letting them see something coming from me to them in their education. Sometimes, I withdrew from my TFSA (Tax Free Savings Account) to pay a part of their school fees. If I cannot buy a house as a woman or mother yet, at least I can participate in building lives which will in turn build me houses. Note what I said, houses.

Working to get monetary resources should not take you away from your children's lives. I had to pick up a part time job when my last child was in primary school in London United Kingdom. I would walk him to school before going to start my part-time job and made sure I got home before he closed from school. As we went to his school together, he would ask me questions about so many topics. We became friends and bonded very well. I was filling the pillow that will give me and my husband comfort in the night time of our lives.

When my children were much younger, I would put baguette (a long, narrow French loaf) with shredded cheese in the oven while waiting for them to come back from school. By the time they arrived, the oven-fresh baguette would be ready, sizzling with melted cheese. They would happily take this with tea or juice. Tell me, whether these children will remember me and my husband in the night of our lives? I was doing this on behalf of myself and my husband who would have gone to work, so we could be comfortable at home. It is worth mentioning that I learnt to make baguette from the school kitchen in the UK where I took on a part-time job.

As soon as my son entered high school and became more autonomous, I took up a full-time job. God is awesome.

God's word is a resource that you cannot place a price on. It is priceless and ever reliable.

A mother who by God's mercies knows the word of God and how to appropriate it in the lives of her children is blessed indeed.

Fill the lives of your children with the word of life that builds and makes life beautiful. What can you do without God's word? Nothing.

A praying mother is a woman of great value. You pray your children into success. There is so much competition out there for limited jobs. You can pray your children to be the most preferred among their peers.

Daniel 6:3

3 Then this Daniel was preferred above the presidents and princes, because an excellent spirit was in him; and the king thought to set him over the whole realm.

You can change a wayward child to become great and bring you comfort in the night of your life.

There are so many ways to pray for your children if you are the type that is limited in prayer ideas. Ask the Holy Spirit to help you and surely, He will.

Get anointed prayer books like (Setting the course of your marriage by Titilayo Akinniyi) and go for mothers' prayer gatherings. Enough of sitting and back-biting while the destinies of our children are in danger. Sit down and do your assignment.

You were created because you were needed. And you know that when women pray, God hears quickly.

Look at the record of Timothy's mother and grandmother in the bible.

<u>2 Timothy 1:5</u>

5 when I call to remembrance the genuine faith that is in you, which dwelt first in your grandmother Lois and your mother Eunice, and I am persuaded is in you also.

Sacrifice

You may have to give up your career or put it on hold for the period of filling your pillow. I had to put my engineering certificate under the bed to focus on the children. If I had to practice like my husband, I would need the help of house helps or relatives. I opted to open a gift shop which gave me the flexibility needed to be with the children.

I have read about some women who gave up their career to nurture the gifts that God has given them (the children).

Please do not abandon your duty post because God is counting on you. There will always be something that you can do around the house or to fit into your children's time that will still bring in enough money to support your husband. A day home, tailoring, online business and blogging if you are good on the computer. There are many things you can do from home. Who told you that God cannot give your husband enough money that will take care of you and the children and even leave surplus to give to the needy? All you need is to pray sincerely for your husband. Your own money will just be for your own use as you wish. Life is sweet and easy. We should not stress ourselves up unnecessarily.

Our children are the only future that we have. Future world peace depends on them.

Knowledge

Knowledge, according to Wikipedia is awareness or understanding of someone or something such as facts, information or skills which is acquired through experience by discovering. It is good to know that discovering takes time and consistency.

To get the right fill for our pillows, we need to know about the different types of fills and their characteristics as previously outlined. We need to know the quantity needed for the shape of the pillow or the size needed for our comfort. If the pillow is wrongly filled, the required comfort may not be achieved. Some pillow fills are soft and firm. They can be shaped as desired while some are not. Some are synthetic which gives off acidic or toxic smell, while some are void of chemicals. Some are cheap while some are expensive. If you are not knowledgeable enough to pick the right fill, you may be creating problem for yourself. The fill that gives out toxic gas, could be very hazardous to health.

Know who your child is. If God has blessed you with more than one, learn each child's temperament. Do not fill them with the same fill. The fill that is okay for the shape of one child may not be suitable for the other child. Remember, pillows come in different forms and shapes. Some children are hyper sensitive while other are not. If you try to enforce some sort of discipline or word of correction on two different children, one may take it in good faith while the other may take it as a demonstration of your hatred. Understand the make of each child. Correct them accordingly to get the full benefit out of them all.

Never show that you love one child more than the other. This is a dangerous game. The despised child of today may be the one that will take care of you in your old age. Preferential treatment among children is not only risky to the parents but also an enemy of unity among the children and generations yet unborn.

Mothers, do not build a house that will be filled with bitterness and anger. Preserve the heritage of God.

CHAPTER 5

Filling Our Pillows

JUST LIKE BUILDING A HOUSE

Houses are built for several reasons, including:

i. To provide a covering (roof) over our heads. The covering keeps us protected from the weather elements. A shelter is a place of security.

ii. To provide safe storage for our belongings. Have you ever seen a man, or a family driven out by the landlord because of financial problems? Such a situation is never a good one. Everything the man and his family have laboured to acquire is thrown outside to be ruined by the rain or sun.

iii. In western countries, the experience is far worse. If a man fails to keep up with his mortgage payments for whatever reason, the house is repossessed by the lender.

No matter how much the man has paid, it will take God for him to come out with something from his investment in the house. None of us shall experience homelessness in Jesus name. It destroys.

iv. To provide a place of rest at night time after a day's work or business activities. Imagine a man having no home to return to at the end of the day's work while others are packing their bags and heading back to their comfortable homes and saying, "see you tomorrow". It is not a good situation to be at all. Conscious effort must be made to build a house that lasts and befits.

Building our pillow takes time and effort for both the woman and indeed for both parents, because it takes the two parents to build successfully with God as their Helper. Remember, nothing great can be achieved outside God.

Before you go into any relationship that you know is meant for marriage, both of you must have adequate knowledge of the responsibilities involved in building restful pillows for your night time.

You do not just start having babies without a solid plan on the ground for their wellbeing. A child that is not well trained will someday sell everything you think you have acquired at a giveaway price.

You must decide how many children you would like to have and make adequate provisions to care for them. Gone are the days when people turn themselves into baby production factories churning out babies and distributing them to relatives to raise on their behalf. Nothing of such happens anymore. Even if you decide to rely on the social welfare in the western world, you will find out sooner or later that the government will only support the child up to secondary school level. What happens after that? Your guess is as good as mine. That is when you see many children going their own ways and becoming a nuisance to the community. Why would you want to be part of the social group that creates problems for the world and themselves? University education is not cheap!

These children never begged to be born and left to face hardship in life. And then you wonder why we have so much crimes in the world. Not training your biological or adopted children is not part of God's plan for anyone.

TAKING RESPONSIBILITY

Filling our pillow can be likened to building a house. Adequate planning is important in any major project or endeavour. In the planning process, consideration must be given to cost, time, personnel, quality and quantity of materials and other factors. Trade-offs are often required where resources are limited or constrained.

You do not want to start your building with unskilled manpower or run out of material and financial resources midway through the project.

Luke 14:28 – 32

28 For which of you, intending to build a tower, does not sit down first and count the cost, whether he has enough to finish it—

29 lest, after he has laid the foundation, and is not able to finish, all who see it begin to mock him,

30 saying, 'This man began to build and was not able to finish'?

31 Or what king, going to make war against another king, does not sit down first and consider whether he is able with ten thousand to meet him who comes against him with twenty thousand?

32 Or else, while the other is still a great way off, he sends a delegation and asks conditions of peace.

Taking responsibility as early as possible for the divine assignment that God has given us in the lives of our children makes life enjoyable for all. We can take charge of the destiny of our children right from the womb or even before conception. Every woman prays to get married and have Godly seeds. If you can see with your mind's eyes, then it will not be difficult for you to pray for your unborn children as a Christian. Sometimes I wish I had been in the light for much longer. One thing I know is that I had a ray of light within me even before I came to the light. How did I know. I knew because as an unbeliever who had just experienced disappointment in a relationship, I remember standing at a spot at the Obalende Police Barracks in Lagos Nigeria where I lived with my mother. There, I made some declarations about the type of husband I would like to marry. I lifted up my eyes as I stood on the dusty ground of the barracks and said, "God I know you are there, all I want from this disappointment is a good husband that will be caring and homely. A husband who will come back from work and sit at the living room watching television with the family or reading newspaper. I desire a husband who will help me in the house and lovingly care for the children". With my faith as tiny as the mustard seed, I did not know that God heard my voice and took notice of me in my sinful state. God granted my heart's desires. Without being told, you could see clearly that God heard me. My husband has indeed been everything that I asked from God - caring, loving and God fearing. I tell single ladies who care to listen to me that if God Almighty could grant me, Titilayo, a sinner, my heart's desire even in my lowly state (faith-wise), then, it is a small matter for God to give them husbands that are better than mine. The scripture says the latter shall be greater than the former. The next generation must be better than the former generation if they are careful to listen to Godly advice form the older ones and act on their advice with the help of the Holy spirit. Whether you become born again early in life or not, God's plan for you will surely come to pass. It may take time though. He waits patiently until you are ready to accept Him as your personal Lord and Saviour. He then illuminates and redirects your steps to the right path for the fulfilment of His purpose in your life. Romans 8:28 - 30 is one my favourite scriptures.

> Romans 8 :28-30
>
> 28 And we know that all things work together for good to those who love God, to those who are the called according to His purpose.
>
> 29 For whom He foreknew, He also predestined to be conformed to the image of His Son, that He might be the firstborn among many brethren.
>
> 30 Moreover whom He predestined, these He also called; whom He called, these He also justified; and whom He justified, these He also glorified.

It is never too early or too late to pray for your children. Start now so you can enjoy a comfortable sleep at night. There is an adage in my native language (Yoruba) that says, "dried fish cannot be bent" (without breaking it). The words in bracket are mine. As true as the adage may sound, I believe it is contrary to the word of God.

The bible says that God is the God of all flesh. Nothing is impossible for Him to do. His word says that the heart of the king is in His hands and He can turn it anywhere He wishes.

Jeremiah 32:27

27 "Behold, I am the Lord, the God of all flesh.
Is there anything too hard for Me?

Proverbs 21:1

The king's heart is in the hand of the Lord,

Like the rivers of water;

He turns it wherever He wishes.

A baby hears the voice of its mother while it is still in the womb. Remember the encounter between Mary, the mother of Jesus and Elisabeth, the mother of John the Baptist. When Mary visited Elisabeth, the bible recorded that as Mary greeted Elisabeth, the baby in Elisabeth's womb leaped.

Luke1:39-42

39 Now Mary arose in those days and went into the hill country with haste, to a city of Judah,

40 and entered the house of Zacharias and greeted Elizabeth.

41 And it happened, when Elizabeth heard the greeting of Mary, that the babe leaped in her womb; and Elizabeth was filled with the Holy Spirit.

42 Then she spoke out with a loud voice and said, "Blessed are you among women, and blessed is the fruit of your womb!

Proclaim aloud what you want to see in your child using the word of God even before you get married. When God looks unto you favourably and counts you worthy to be rewarded with the fruit of the womb, do not take God's mercy for granted. Don't just keep quiet, go ahead and wash the cover and inner parts of your pillow with the word of God.

There is tremendous power in the tongue. Life and death are in the power of the tongue.

> Proverbs 18:21
>
> 21 Death and life are in the power of the tongue,
>
> And those who love it will eat its fruit.

Use your God-given power to fill your pillow for a good night's rest.

PUTTING IN ALL THE CARE

No amount of care you put into your pillow is too much. In fact, you must put in all you can to make your pillow fit for your use. If you neglect your pillow, two or more things are bound to happen to it.

1. It may be trampled on by people passing by.
2. It may be stolen from you, leaving you naked.

When the value of a thing is not known, then abuse is inevitable. It is possible for you to abuse the gift of God in your life. The children are God's gifts, not man's gifts. He gives as

He desires. For some couples, these gifts come on a platter of gold. They made no effort to get the gifts. The children just started coming as soon as they got married. They never had to fast or pray before getting the gifts from God. So, they see no reason why they should put in the extra effort to care for their pillows. They take things for granted. This is a gross abuse of God's great gifts.

Some people had to wait for a long time fasting and praying to God before the children started to arrive. They had to spend money and time before they got their gifts. These set of people do not need much counsel before embarking on the needful task of caring for their pillows. Someone said, if you know how to think, you will know how to thank. Caring for your pillow from the very first day of receiving them from God, shows your appreciation and gratitude to the Giver of good and perfect gifts.

The word of God is the absolute foundation of our caring.

Acts 20:32

32 "So now, brethren, I commend you to God and to the word of His grace, which is able to build you up and give you an inheritance among all those who are sanctified.

SEARCH FOR KNOWLEDGE

No one would intentionally want to sleep at night with his head on an uncomfortable pillow. Most of the time, the issue with people is ignorance, lack of money or I don't care attitude. Just like what I said earlier, the search for knowledge of who our children are cannot be over emphasised. What you do not know will always be your boss. Go all out for knowledge.

Hosea 4:6

My people are destroyed for lack of knowledge.

Because you have rejected knowledge,

I also will reject you from being priest for Me;

Because you have forgotten the law of your God,

I also will forget your children.

A SOFT TEXTURE FOR OUR PILLOW COVER

Note that being soft does not mean weakness. It only connotes care for others. As parents, we must be able to infuse into the lives or subconscious mind of our children the importance of caring for other people.

Philippians 2:4

4 Let each of you look out not only for his own interests, but also for the interests of others.

Love or care is the binding agent of the society. A careless society is a doomed society. Caring starts from the home. Remember that home is the base or the foundation of any community or nation. If the foundation be destroyed what can the righteous do?

Psalms 3:11

If the foundations are destroyed, What can the righteous do?

A child that lacks care and love or the knowledge of love from a tender age may find it difficult to give anybody any kind of care or love. What you do not have you cannot give. When a child becomes so addicted to a toy that he or she cannot share it with others, the parents should be quick to rescue that child. You may say that he or she is only a child, but the mind of little children is like a mould. Whatever you pour into it is what you get. A child picks up a speaking accent of his environment no matter the colour of his or her skin. A child does not have to be of a colour or tribe or class before picking up the tongue of the people around him or her. It only takes a little exposure of the child to the people around.

The company you keep determines what accompanies you.

What is seen outwardly is determined by what is inside. A good man, out of the good things in his heart flings out good treasure and a bad man out of the bad things in his heart brings out bad things. There is no two way about it.

Matthew 12:34

34 Brood of vipers! How can you, being evil, speak good things? For out of the abundance of the heart the mouth speaks.

Parents should make conscious effort to fill the hearts of their children with good things that will make the outer cover of their pillow soft and attractive to good and pleasant things for the benefit of all.

Let's look at it this way. For our skins to look great, we feed well on balanced diets. There are some types of food like fatty fish such as salmon, mackerel and herring and other foods like Avocados, walnuts, sunflower seeds, sweet potatoes, red or yellow pepper and broccoli that are high in healthy fats and are excellent foods for healthy skin. They are also recommended for good nails and hair. Maintaining the health of our body, including the skin, does not depend mainly on the type of body cream, hair shampoo or nail cream that we use. If we take time to be good food selectors, we may not have to spend a fortune on what we apply to the outer part of our bodies. You see? Feeding the inside well brings out a glow on the outside. The beauty within will always produce a glow on the outside.

The saying that charity begins at home is very true. Charity with what our mind feeds on will lead to softness and glowing of our character outside.

You could tell what is inside a child within a few minutes of meeting the child. What the child is made of and what type of investment the parents made in the child's upbringing is visible on the outside.

Someone said, spending just the first few minutes with a child or wife reveals who the parents or husband is.

Nothing can be truer than this statement.

God has given us the power to perceive and know what is going on around us or what the person we are with or dealing with is made of.

Parents should be asking themselves the following questions:

- What is the world beholding in our children?
- What covering do we have on our children?
- What is the covering made of?
- What is the texture of the fabric that makes the covering on our children?

It is very clear from our discussions about fabric and pillow covering that parents need to carefully and prayerfully select what their children are fed on at home. When I say fed on, I am not referring to food. The fact remains that what you eat determines to a large extent what your skin looks like as mentioned. If you take in junk food always, your skin becomes rough and unpleasant because you are feeding your skin on dangerous radicals.

The word of our mouth is like food. It either nourishes or damages the body. The bible says in

Proverbs 25:11

11 A word fitly spoken is like apples of gold
In settings of silver.

Our words in the lives of our children reflect on their outward look or behaviour. How do I mean? A child that is addressed roughly or criticised openly in the presence of friends will either revolt against the parents or curl up in a shell of low self-esteem. In this way, we have created an ugly situation or covering for the child. No amount of word of encouragement given to the child will make much change because he or she has been injured emotionally by the most trusted person in his or her life. We must be very careful of what we say, how we say it and when we say it to our children. This goes a long way in the lives of our children. Correcting in love is very important.

We should not exempt our children from correction, but we should correct them in love.

<u>Proverbs 29:15</u>

"The rod and rebuke give wisdom, but a child
left to himself brings shame to his mother."

Let the child know the reason for the punishment. The story was told of a boy who was woken up by his father in the middle of the night and beaten because of an offence he committed during the day. When he was asked by his father if he knew why he was being punished, his innocent response was, "you beat me because I was sleeping". See? Timely correction in love with full explanation boosts the inner strength and sharpens the outer colour of the child.

Remember, the computer language "Garbage in, garbage out". Whatever you deposit in a child's life will reflect on the outside and could be embarrassing to the parents sometimes. Unattractive outward cover is repelling. It can take destiny helpers away from your child. Do you want success for your children? Their success is your success. If they are great and have all round success in marriage, career, spiritual life and all that makes life enjoyable, you will not only be a proud parent but comfortable as well and singing on your way to heaven thanking God for Godly and goodly children.

Our words of correction to the children should be guided by the scriptures. We must be in partnership with God to nurture them in the way of God. Remember, we are only channels that facilitate their journey through life. We did not give them life. We did not decide their gender or assignment in life. They are the heritage of God.

Psalm127:3

3 Behold, children are a heritage from the Lord,

The fruit of the womb is a reward.

Which means, God is the one in control of our children's lives, but He relies on us here on earth to partner with Him for His plan and purpose for them to be fulfilled. We need divine vision receptors for the selection of the fabric of our pillows.

WASHING OUR DIRTY PILLOW

A natural pillow may become dirty if not properly used or become flattened from long use. The good thing is that it can be restored when it goes bad. So also, the pillow of our lives, the children, can be 'reshaped' when they go out of the plan and purpose of God.

> ### Matthew 19:26
>
> 26 But Jesus looked at them and said to them, "With men this is impossible, but with God all things are possible."

When the normal pillow becomes dirty, you can wash it with water. The following steps could be taken when washing a dirty pillow.

i.   Remove the cover.
ii. Fill a tub with water.
iii. Add your detergent.
iv. Wash the pillow.
v.   Rinse the pillow.
vi. Dry the pillow.
vii. Check the pillow.

Let us see how we can apply these steps to our pillows (our children).

Never lose hope on a child that is wayward or seemingly out of control.

The first thing to do is to remove the outer cover that represents the visible dirtiness in the life of the child. It makes the child unattractive to helpers of destiny. It disassociates the child from the company of great achievers.

How do we remove this cover? You do this by the word of God spoken from your mouth.

Zechariah 3:1- 4

1 Then he showed me Joshua the high priest standing before the Angel of the Lord, and Satan standing at his right hand to oppose him.

2 And the Lord said to Satan, "The Lord rebuke you, Satan! The Lord who has chosen Jerusalem rebuke you! Is this not a brand plucked from the fire?"

3 Now Joshua was clothed with filthy garments, and was standing before the Angel.

4 Then He answered and spoke to those who stood before Him, saying, "Take away the filthy garments from him." And to him He said, "See, I have removed your iniquity from you, and I will clothe you with rich robes."

Fill the lives of your children with the word of life that can turn an ugly situation to an attractive one. If you look beyond the dirty cover on your child and continue to speak the word of God into his/her life every day, you will start to see changes in the child's behaviour and a glow on the outside. Hallelujah.

Ephesians 5:26

26 that He might sanctify and cleanse her with the washing of water by the word,

Nothing washes clean like the word of God. The word of God is powerful, quick and can penetrate any situation that may look impenetrable.

Soak your child in the word of God by creating time to study the word with him or her regularly. As you do this, the word is gaining access to the heart and transformation is taking place outside and inside.

Hebrews 4:12

12 For the word of God is living and powerful, and sharper than any two-edged sword, piercing even to the division of soul and spirit, and of joints and marrow, and is a discerner of the thoughts and intents of the heart.

As you make it a habit to speak the word of God into your child's life through prayer and daily confessions, you will be rinsing out the bad fills from his life, making the child to be rid of bad character and giving way to Godly character.

Drying the pillow removes any form of moisture that may lead to the growth of bacteria. Bacteria is known to thrive best on moist surfaces. Be sure that your child is completely dried from the bad influences in his life by making sure that he or she keeps good company and is surrounded by the people who genuinely love him or her.

You keep checking that the right temperature is maintained around the child. Never assume that the child is okay and leave him alone. The tendency to go back to a dirty life is always there. As much as we do not want to overburden our children with our monitoring, we should not allow them to be alone without checking on the temperature of the word of God in their lives. The fire on our prayer altar must keep burning.

Leviticus 6:13

13 A fire shall always be burning on the altar; it shall never go out.

DEADLINE FOR FILLING OUR PILLOW

If we are still alive and the children are there, we must keep filling our pillow if we want a restful night. If you are trying to cut a tree and you stop midway, you have not achieved anything. No result or proof. Filling your pillow is a continuous task and no time is too much. Whatever we pay attention to regularly will always remain good and useful. Filling our pillow on a continuous basis is like maintaining the pillow.

It is like eating, and making sure we eat right every day. In this analogy, the food is our prayer and the conscious efforts we make to see that our pillow is in good condition.

THE BEAUTY OF GOOD PILLOW FILL

- It is comfortable
- It is heathy because it has no toxic gas
- It preserves lives and destinies especially those of parents in their old age.

- It makes night time rest enjoyable.
- It is rewarding.
- It lasts and gives value for money spent.

Remember that good pillows are the gifts of God to us, but what we make out of these gifts will determine how our night times in life will be.

God is the giver of good and perfect gifts.

<u>James 1:17</u>

17 Every good gift and every perfect gift is from above, and comes down from the Father of lights, with whom there is no variation or shadow of turning.

The children that God gives us are good and perfect gifts.

Sometimes we make the perfect children to turn to imperfect ones by the way we train them or our attitudes to them. Let's not be careless about raising our children.

SIDE EFFECTS OF USING UNSUITABLE FILLS

i. Insomnia. That is not having enough sleep. Restlessness. This brings irritability. We may be feeling very uncomfortable at night. May our children not be the source of insomnia at the night of our lives in Jesus name. Thinking about the child that is in the police custody or prison may be the source of sleeplessness to the parents. Nothing makes life more difficult than a wayward child with criminal mind. It is very painful and shameful. No matter who you are or how rich you are, if your child is always in the police web, your night sleep may not be so sweet. That shall not be your portion in Jesus name.

The bible says that God gives His beloved sleep.

Psalm 127:2

2 It is vain for you to rise up early,

To sit up late,

To eat the bread of sorrows;

For so He gives His beloved sleep.

That is very true as we all know that the word of God is true and God cannot lie. The question now is, what do we do to be able to partake of this promise. We need to hearken to God's instruction on how to train our children to avoid sleeplessness.

ii. Cervical spondylosis or neck arthritis. This is waking up with pain in the neck and is a common, age-related condition that affects the joints and discs in the cervical spine, which is in the neck. It develops from the wear and tear of cartilage and bones. There are discs in the spinal bones which are like thick, pad like cushions that absorb the shock of lifting and twisting. When the discs are not there or worn out, it brings pain. Our children being filled with the right fills as pillows are the discs that absorb our pain at the night time of our lives. Some spinal cords are lacking the necessary discs. It is my prayer that our discs shall not be worn out when we most need them for comfort in Jesus name.

iii. Waking up with headaches. A headache can be a sign of stress or emotional distress. When the night time is not restful, it can lead to many abnormalities in the body. The body is not at its best condition and the body system becomes disorderly.

Unsuitable pillow fills can be very discomforting. It is not what anybody wants after the day's work and all you are praying for is good sleep. Lack of sleep could be an invitation to sickness or disease.

Our night time shall not be filled with pains and sleeplessness in Jesus name.

When you do what God says to do in the lives of the children that He gave you, your nights will be comfortable and full of peaceful rest.

Do not fill your pillows with stones or chaff. Remember, some pillow fills give out toxic gases that may snuff life out of the user.

When we partner with God diligently, not leaving our responsibilities to others, our neck will rest comfortably on the pillow and our night time will be very sweet and comfortable.

It is my prayer that God in His mercies will equip every parent with what it takes to identify the right cover material for their children and the right fill material to fill them for the benefit of the parents and the whole world.

Parents, let God see you as the great partner in the job of training your child.

PUTTING IT INTO PRACTICE

Be there for the children.

1. Have quality time with your female child as a father.

2. Teach your son to be responsible domestically and spiritually. Teach him to love women with the love of Christ, not lusting after them. He should be taught to value women and not to abuse or disrespect them. As parents especially mothers, we should remember that the son that we trained to love and respect people, especially women, will bring praise and glory to us. Not only that, he will tell the story to his wife and the result will be respect and care for her husband's parents. Genuine true story is sweet and soothing to our soul and spirit.

3. Mothers should be close to the female children too, teaching them early in life how to keep themselves as the temple of God, staying pure and undefiled, keeping themselves for their husbands only. Not to be carried away by material things or temporary comfort given by any man who is not their husbands. Teach them to have control over their appetite, not to be lured into ungodly relationships through food. Many destinies have been

destroyed because of free fast food or restaurant visits offered by men with bad intentions.

Proverbs 23:1 – 3

1 When you sit down to eat with a ruler,

Consider carefully what is before you;

2 And put a knife to your throat

If you are a man given to appetite.

3 Do not desire his delicacies,

For they are deceptive food.

4. If it is within your power, show the female children how to value people but not to be attracted to what people have. That is, to be content with what they have and never to compare themselves with anybody or allow anyone to intimidate them in any way or form. Take them out to places you think a man may use to lure them to do what is not right like having sex with them. Take them to hotels and spend some time together as a family, exposing them to what makes life attractive and comfortable in your own little way. You do not have to travel abroad, there are places of interest near you that you can invest in. Even if it is watching rented movies together, just do something to destroy the spirit of lust or covetousness in their lives.

5. Above all, teach your children to fear God and respect people. Remember that the fear of God is the beginning

of wisdom and wisdom is the preserving ingredient in anyone's life.

Proverbs 9:10

10 "The fear of the Lord is the beginning of wisdom,

And the knowledge of the Holy One is understanding.

CHAPTER 6

Let Us Pray

PRAYER FOR OUR CHILDREN

1. Father in the name of Jesus make my children my crown of glory in the night of my life.
2. Father, in the name of Jesus let my children be eternal excellency and the joy of many generations bringing joy to the hearts of many including me in Jesus name.
3. Father, in the name of Jesus make my joy to be full concerning my children all the days of my life, nothing broken nothing missing in their destinies in Jesus name.

Get more prayers for the children from the book: Setting the course of your marriage by Titilayo Akinniyi.

PRAYER FOR OURSELVES AS PARENTS

1. Father in the name of Jesus make my life count in the destinies of my children.
2. Father, in the name of Jesus let me not be an instrument of destruction to the glorious destinies of my children through physical, spiritual or sexual abuse.
3. Father, make me an active parent in channelling my children's lives in the right direction.

May the grace and wisdom of God be made available to all parents to fill their pillows with the right fill that will make their sleep at the night of their lives comfortable and may they enjoy the fruits of their labour in peace in Jesus name.

CPSIA information can be obtained
at www.ICGtesting.com
Printed in the USA
BVHW070916170419
545787BV00003B/508/P

9 781796 025378